THIS BOOK IS A GIFT OF:

FRIENDS OF THE
LAFAYETTE LIBRARY

Contra Costa County Library

The Biggest Animal On Land

By Allan Fowler

Consultants

Robert L. Hillerich, Professor Emeritus,
Bowling Green State University, Bowling Green, Ohio;
Consultant, Pinellas County Schools, Florida

Lynne Kepler, Educational Consultant

Fay Robinson, Child Development Specialist

Children's Press®
A Division of Grolier Publishing
New York   London   Hong Kong   Sydney
Danbury, Connecticut

Project Editor: Downing Publishing Services
Designer: Herman Adler Design Group
Photo Researcher: Feldman & Associates, Inc.

Library of Congress Cataloging-in-Publication Data

Fowler, Allan.
 The biggest animal on land / by Allan Fowler.
   p. cm. – (Rookie read-about science)
 Includes index.
 Summary: An introduction to the elephant, the biggest animal on land.
 ISBN 0-516-06050-3
  1. Elephants—Juvenile literature. 2. Zoo animals—Juvenile literature.
 [1. Elephants.] I. Title. II. Series.
QL737.P98F68   1996
599.6'1–dc20   95-39674
                                                   CIP
                                                    AC

The biggest animal on land is also one of the smartest . . .

one of the gentlest . . . and
one of the most popular.

Almost everyone enjoys
watching elephants. After
all, there's so much to like.

Elephants are bigger than
any other animal that lives
on land.

And they certainly have
the longest noses —
their trunks.

An elephant breathes
through its trunk . . .
and even uses its trunk
to feed itself.

Have you ever seen an elephant pick up a big bundle of hay, or a tiny peanut, with its trunk — and then put it in its mouth?

Or squirt water or sand
on its back to get rid of
pesky flies?

If an elephant has
ears as big as these —
then you know it's an
African elephant.

Indian elephants are not quite as large as African elephants — and their ears are much smaller.

Most of the elephants
you see in zoos and
circuses are Indian.

Elephants in the wild travel in groups called herds.

Baby elephants, or calves, are very hairy when they are born.

They quickly lose their hair. But they keep feeding on their mothers' milk for three or four years.

An elephant takes about as long as you do to reach its full size.

It lives about 60 years.

How smart are elephants?
Very smart. They are
taught to perform clever
tricks at the circus.

And in Asia they haul
heavy loads and do other
useful work.

Elephants can run very fast.

They also swim well while they hold their trunks above the water to breathe.

An elephant's tusks are
really very long teeth.

All African elephants
have tusks. Male Indian
elephants have them,
but not the females.

Elephant's tusks are
made of ivory.

23

Artists have carved ivory.
It used to be made into
piano keys.

Hunters used to kill many
elephants for their ivory.

This had to be stopped,
or soon there might
not be any elephants
left in the wild.

Laws protect the elephants now.

Large pieces of land have been set aside as game preserves.

Elephants and other endangered animals can live there without being hunted.

There should always be lots of elephants!

Words You Know

African elephant

Indian elephant

herd

calf

trunks

ivory

tusks

Index

About the Author

Allan Fowler is a free-lance writer with a background in advertising. Born in New York, he lives in Chicago now and enjoys traveling.

Photo Credits